CONTENTS

The power plant of the DBR1. This six-cylinder, 2.9-litre engine produced a very modest 240 bhp at a time when 3-litre V12 Ferraris were giving a fairly honest 300 bhp . . .

Introduction

Aston Martin is one of the most charismatic names in the motoring catalogue. Throughout its long and unsettled history the company has produced numerous beautiful and exciting sporting cars in small numbers, the majority of which still survives and prospers, thanks in no small way to the enthusiasm generated by the Aston Martin Owners Club.

In this book we have attempted to illustrate most – but by no means all – of the models built by Aston Martin since 1915 and to give a brief, but accurate history of the company, which has now found a secure home within the Ford Motor Co. We have also taken a good look at the AMOC and Ecurie Bertelli, which sustain Astons' racing heritage so magnificently.

For their help in this venture we would like to thank our friends at Aston Martin Lagonda, Ltd; Alan Archer – Archivist and former President of the Aston Martin Owners Club – for availing us of his unrivalled knowledge of both the company and the Club; Judy Hogg of Ecurie Bertelli and Steve Earle of the Monterey Historic race meeting in California.

Chris Nixon & Richard Newton

Sisters under the skin. A rare, DB Mk III Fixed Head Coupé of 1959 takes off on a lap of Silverstone in company with a brand-new Virage. The former of the property of the AMOC's Deputy Chairman, Ian MacGregor

ASTON MARTIN
Heritage

Chris Nixon

Richard Newton

OSPREY
AUTOMOTIVE

First published in 1991 by
Osprey Publishing Limited
59 Grosvenor Street
London W1X 9DA

British Library Cataloguing in Publication
Data
Nixon, Chris
 Aston Martin Heritage
 I. Aston Martin sports cars
 I. Title II. Newton, Richard
 629·2'3
ISBN 0850 45964 8

Text: Chris Nixon
Photography: Richard Newton
Editor: Colin Burnham
Page design: Angela Posen

Phototypeset by Keyspools Ltd, Warrington
Printed in Hong Kong

Title page
*A Le Mans 2/4 seater – with matching
wire stone-guards on radiator and
headlamps, with the Ecurie Bertelli
cars in the background*

Half title page
Tail-end Charlies?

Back cover
*David Acon's beautiful 1933 Le Mans
in action during the St. John Horsfall
Trophy Race*

For a catalogue of all books published by Osprey Automotive
please write to:

**The Marketing Department,
Octopus Illustrated Books, 1st Floor, Michelin House,
81 Fulham Road, London SW3 6RB**

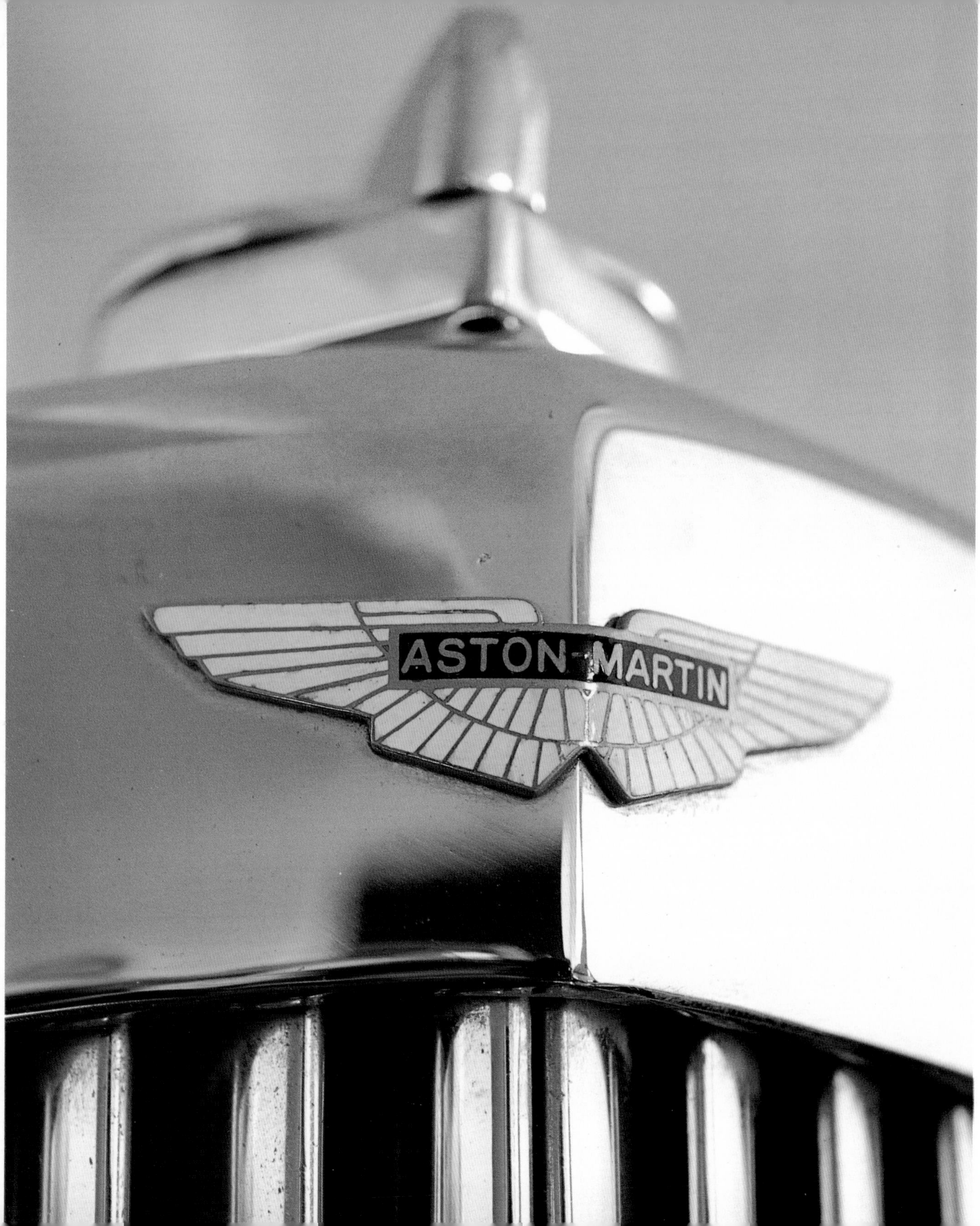
ASTON-MARTIN

Aston Martin – The Great Survivor

Arguably the most remarkable thing about the marque Aston Martin is that it is still with us. Since 1914, when Lionel Martin and his partner, Robert Bamford, decided to build and market a light car known as Aston-Martin (with a hyphen), numerous people and companies have repeatedly snatched the marque from impending oblivion, convinced that it could be turned into a profit-making concern.

It is almost certainly true to say that each failed in this endeavour until Victor Gauntlett arrived on the scene in 1980, and he did not enjoy seeing black numerals in Aston Martin's financial statements where previously there had only been red until some time in 1988. Yet despite running at a loss for almost all its life, Aston Martin has survived where other, temporarily more successful firms have failed and now, having entered the last decade of the century as part of the giant Ford Motor Co., appears to be thoroughly secure for the very first time.

The firm of Bamford and Martin began in 1913, operating as agents for Singer cars in South-East England. After modifying one of these machines to increase its performance, Lionel Martin took part in some trials and hillclimbs and a few races at Brooklands. As a result, several people asked him to modify their Singers in similar fashion, which prompted him to think about designing a car of his own. In order to try out his ideas, he had an engine built for him by Coventry-Simplex which he fitted into an Isotta-Fraschini chassis, prior to completing the first car to bear his own name in 1915.

However, instead of calling his creation a Martin, he named it Aston-Martin and the reason for this appears to be two-fold. His wife, Katherine (who later became a director of Bamford and Martin) reasoned that if her husband was going to build and sell motor cars it would be no bad thing to give them a name that would appear high on any alphabetical list of makes. Lionel had competed successfully with his Singer at a climb on Aston Hill, near Tring in Buckinghamshire, so Aston was an ideal choice.

The first Aston-Martin remained the only Aston-Martin until late in 1920, as plans for production were thwarted by the First World War, but in that year the company moved to 53 Abingdon Road, Kensington, in London, where some sixty cars were built during the

A Virage chassis takes shape under a welder's torch

next half-a-dozen years. (The precise number is not known.)

By 1924 Bamford and Martin was in deep financial trouble. The company was briefly rescued by Lady Charnwood, but late in 1925 it was in the hands of the Official Receiver. The following year Lord Charnwood, together with William Renwick and A. C. Bertelli, bought the assets of Bamford and Martin and set up a new firm, Aston Martin Motors, Ltd, at a new premises in Victoria Road, Feltham, Middlesex. Phase Two of the Aston Martin saga had begun.

It became known as the Bertelli era. 'Bert' Bertelli was an Italian-born engineer who knew the value of competition, and once the new production Aston Martin (now without the hyphen) was underway he prepared two racing versions for the 1928 Le Mans 24-hour race, giving the chassis the prefix LM, which all his factory racing cars would carry.

The new production car was called the International and proved to

A line-up of skeletal Virages at Newport Pagnell. Each one already has an owner, who has specified the colour of paint and interior trim

be a great success, but the Wall Street crash of 1929 badly affected sales. By now Bertelli was running the company (which had become Aston Martin, Ltd) and in 1931 he secured a remarkable arrangement with H. J. Aldington of Frazer Nash, who not only agreed to sell Aston Martins but also to finance the building of three new racing cars.

Later, a London car dealer named Lance Prideaux-Brune offered to buy into Aston Martin, Ltd. Bertelli seized upon this as a way of paying off Aldington and building three more racers. Sales did not improve, however, and within a year Prideaux-Brune had to withdraw from the company. In true Aston Martin fashion, another wealthy benefactor emerged almost at once, in the form of wealthy industrialist Sir Arthur Sutherland. He bought the company and made his son, Gordon, joint Managing Director with Bertelli.

The very successful International model was succeeded by the Le

Above
Even at this early stage, the elegant lines of John Heffernan and Ken Greenley's bodyshape are becoming apparent

Right
A Virage roof is beaten into shape by hand before being fitted to the chassis. The noise is deafening

Mans and the Mk II, which came in 2, 2/4 and 4-seater form. These 1.5-litre Astons were among the finest sports/touring cars of their day and many were sold on the strength of the factory's racing programme, but not enough. In 1936 Gordon Sutherland (a keen racing enthusiast) reluctantly came to the conclusion that Astons could not survive on sports cars alone, as the market simply was not big enough. He decided that the company's next product should be a sports saloon and that Aston Martin should pull out of racing. These decisions were undoubtedly correct, but they went against everything 'Bert' Bertelli stood for and in 1937 he resigned from the company, a disillusioned man. Another Aston Martin era was over.

With the aid of engineer Claude Hill (who had been with Astons since the 1920s) Gordon Sutherland produced his new car, the Two Litre 15/98. This was based on the Speed Model built for the 1936 Le Mans, which had been cancelled. The 15/98 was a commercial success and Hill then used it as the basis for a new Speed Model, the Type C, but it was given a very ugly body and its performance was no better than the earlier machine. Only a handful was sold and then the outbreak of World War Two brought all production to a halt.

During the war, Claude Hill was somehow able to work on a new model, which was dubbed 'The Atom'. This had a tubular chassis and a 15/98 engine which was later replaced by a new 2-litre unit designed by Hill. The Atom showed great promise, but the advent of peace in 1945 did not bring any money in its wake with which to develop the car. At the end of 1946 an un-named car company was advertised for sale in *The Times*. Once again, Aston Martin was looking for a new owner.

On this occasion it was millionaire industrialist, David Brown (now Sir David), who took up the challenge and in February, 1947 he bought Aston Martin for £20,000. Later in the year he was persuaded to buy the Lagonda company as well, although the only thing about it that really interested him was the new, 2.6-litre, six-cylinder, twin-ohc engine which had been designed by the great W. O. Bentley. Having bought both firms, he moved them into the old aircraft hangars at Hanworth Park, Feltham and the DB era began.

A new Aston Martin, based on the chassis of Hill's Atom, went on sale at the 1948 Earls Court Motor Show, where it was known as the Two-Litre Sports model. It had a good-looking body designed by Frank Feeley (who had come to Astons from Lagonda) but David Brown was not impressed with Hill's push-rod, 2-litre engine. Having bought Lagonda expressly to get his hands on the twin overhead camshaft unit, he abandoned Hill's design in favour of Bentley's. The result was a big row with a very aggrieved Hill, who left the

The Virage will appear in three forms: the 'basic' saloon; the Volante drophead coupé and the superfast Vantage. This is a prototype Volante in the making

Once completed, the chassis are covered in corrosion-resistant paint

company, as did Gordon Sutherland. David Brown then commissioned a new car, to be called the DB2. The Sports model became known retrospectively as the DB1.

Claude Hill's excellent chassis was given a beautiful, streamlined body by Frank Feeley and, powered by the 2.6-litre Lagonda engine, the DB2 became an instant classic. More than 1700 examples of this car and its variants were built between 1950 and 1959, by which time it was known as the DB Mk III and powered by a 2.9-litre engine. At the end of its life it was being built not at Feltham, but at the Tickford Works at Newport Pagnell, which David Brown had acquired in 1953, moving production there in 1957.

That same year, David Brown appointed John Wyer as Technical Director of what was now Aston Martin Lagonda, Ltd. Wyer had been Team Manager in charge of Astons' Competition Department since 1950 and he brought a much-needed orderliness to Aston Martin's production line. He made Harold Beach (who had also joined the company in 1950) Chief Designer and set about replacing the ageing DB Mk III with a completely new model.

Frank Feeley had left Aston Martin and Wyer decided to go to Italy for his new body design, which was produced to stunning effect by Carrozzeria Touring of Milan. Designated the DB4, the new car was powered by a 3.7-litre straight-six engine designed by Tadek Marek, an expatriate Pole who had joined Astons in 1953. This unit went into the DB5 and DB6, until it was superseded by Marek's masterpiece, the 5.3-litre V8, which appeared in the DBS (not, for some reason, the DB7) in 1969. Twenty years on this magnificent engine – in its latest, four-valve form – is the power behind the superb new Virage.

The DBS had a new body designed by William Towns and – in V8 form – was the last of the David Brown Astons. Since 1953 the Aston Martin badge had incorporated its owner's name and for more than twenty years the prestige generated by the very expensive, high-performance Grand Touring cars – coupled with the success of the racing team throughout the world – had provided a very valuable publicity spin-off for the David Brown Tractor Co. and the parent company, the David Brown Gear Co., of Huddersfield, in Yorkshire – but at a price.

Sir David reckons that Aston Martin ran at a loss of around £1,000,000 per year during his ownership and there came a time when this was no longer acceptable. In 1972 the David Brown Corporation as a whole was badly hit by the recession and Aston Martin Lagonda, Ltd was sold to Company Developments, Ltd for a nominal £1, as the new owner was taking over a very large debt.

The next two years saw Aston Martin come closer than ever to

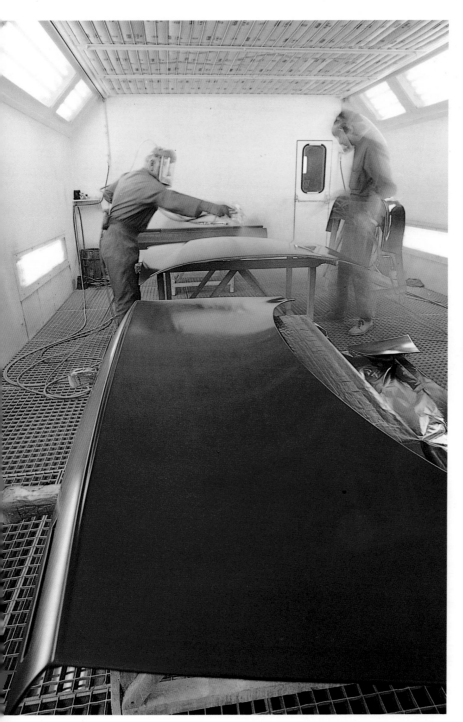

Above

Careful masking ensures that paint goes only where it is needed

Left

A Virage bonnet is sprayed by hand in carefully controlled conditions

Every car undergoes this infra-red treatment, which drives the water particles out of the paint and helps prevent corrosion. Astons were the first car manufacturer to use this system

extinction and at the end of 1974 the factory was closed and the Official Receiver took over. It really did look like the end of the road, but yet again Aston Martin refused to lie down and die. This time it found four saviours: Alan Curtis, Peter Sprague, George Minden and Denis Flather, and under their management, production got under way again with the V8.

In May, 1980, Victor Gauntlett joined the Board and took a 10 per cent share in the company. By December he was co-owner, with Tim Hearley of CH Industrials, Ltd. During the next three years things went from bad to worse until, in the summer of 1984, Gauntlett was able to persuade the American-based Greek shipping magnate, George Livanos, through his aunt Irene's family trust to buy 75 per cent of Aston Martin Lagonda, Ltd. George's son, Peter, was already involved in the company and he and Gauntlett had only recently instigated a very successful, limited edition Aston Martin with styling by Zagato, the company which had produced a stunning body for the DB4GT, back in 1960.

Taking shape. A V8 engine in the process of being built, a one-man operation which takes between 60–70 hours

Above
Where the power comes in. A couple of V8s and several gearboxes are given a final check before being fitted into their Virage chassis. Especially designed to meet emission control requirements world-wide, the 32-valve, all-alloy V8 produces 330 bhp at 6000 rpm and 340 lb/ft of torque at 3700 rpm. Power is transmitted through a five-speed manual gearbox

Right
The V8 is a very snug fit in the engine bay

The Livanos family's very large financial commitment provided the lifeboat which, with Gauntlett at the helm, kept Aston Martin afloat until September, 1987, when the Ford Motor Co. came to the rescue and purchased the Livanos shares. The other 25 per cent were retained by Gauntlett and Peter Livanos.

Ever since he had joined the company, Victor Gauntlett had recognised the need for a completely new car to replace the V8 and its Volante, Vantage and Zagato variants, and well before the sale to Ford was on the cards he had courageously commissioned the first new Aston for twenty years. Under the supervision of Deputy Chief Executive Bill Bannard and Engineering Manager Rob Robinson, the car was produced in just two years and the Virage – with elegant bodywork by John Heffernan and Ken Greenley – made its debut at the SMMT Motor Show in 1989, to universal acclaim.

Fears that Ford might ruin Aston Martin by dragging it downmarket and producing Aston Sierras or Cortinas have, mercifully, proved groundless. The new parent company is determined to continue producing exclusive, high-performance Aston Martins and, surprisingly perhaps, made no attempt to impose its views on the Virage. It did, however, make its vast wealth of technology available to Astons and a very good relationship has grown up between the people at Newport Pagnell and Dearborn.

After seventy-five years of teetering on the high-wire of uncertainty, Aston Martin has at last achieved a secure base on which to build for the future. The Virage and the drop-head Volante are now coming off the production line at the rate of six a week and will shortly be joined by Astons' supercar, the Virage Vantage – a twin supercharged beauty producing some 480 bhp and over 500 lb/ft of torque, giving it a performance in the Ferrari F40 range.

Looking ahead to the middle of the decade, Victor Gauntlett's plans for a smaller, less expensive Aston are well under way. 'Less expensive' is a relative term of course, and in this case means a price-tag of perhaps two-thirds that of the Virage which, at the time of writing, is £125,000. But Gauntlett is adamant that it will be a true Aston Martin, powered by a smaller version of Tadek Marek's great V8 and having bodywork made up of aluminium pressings, rather than being coach-built like the Virage. A new factory will be needed to produce these at the rate of almost 1000 cars per year.

For a company that has its origins in the humble, 10 hp Singer way back in 1913, Aston Martin has done pretty well, despite the many dramas along the way. Lionel Martin would surely be delighted with the current state of his creation, and its bright prospects for the future.

Further up the production line, with cars nearing completion

Two Virages being given a last-minute check before taking to the roads of Newport Pagnell for a test run. The red car is already carrying trade plates

The finished product. Sixteen weeks after it was begun, a new Virage is ready for delivery

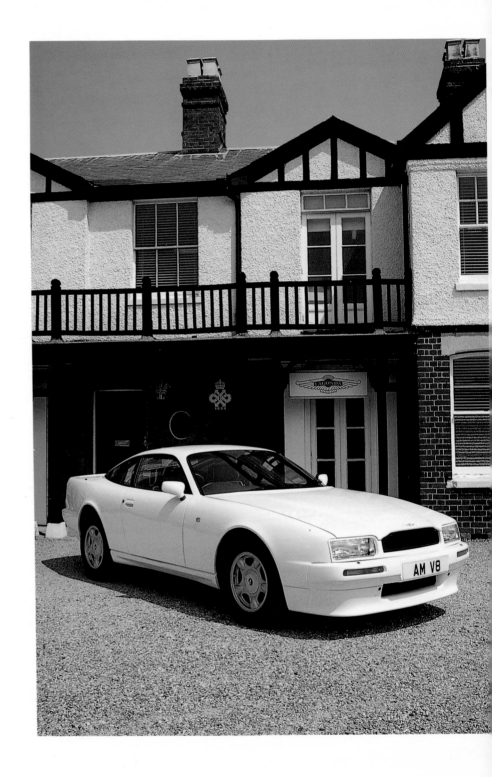

Once David Brown had acquired the company in 1947, he sent stylist Frank Feeley to Italy for inspiration. Upon his return to Feltham, Feeley drew the timeless DB2, a drophead version of which is seen here. Initially, the radiator grille was in three parts

With the arrival of the DB2/4 in
1953, Feeley blended the three grilles
into one

In March, 1957, the DB2/4 Mk III
made its debut at the Geneva Show. It
was Frank Feeley's swansong for Aston
Martin and he gave it a grille similar
to that on his masterpiece, the racing
DB3S

When Carrozzeria Touring produced the stunning DB4 in 1958 they refined Feeley's grille still further and continued it through the DB5 and DB6 models

Faired-in headlamps became a feature
of the Touring bodies. This is a Volante

The DBS of 1967 was designed by William Towns, who extended the grille to include the headlamps. In doing so he lost much of the Aston's identity

With the end of the David Brown era in 1972, Towns re-discovered the intrinsic shape of the grille with the V8

The dramatic V8 Vantage had no need of an air scoop on the bonnet and the grille was blanked off

*Astons' latest stylists, John Heffernan
and Ken Greenly, refined Frank
Feeley's original grille shape still
further for the Virage, but a shape is
all it is. The air intake is below the
number plate*

Above and right
Italian variations: Zagato's DB4GT of 1960 was stunning. The V8 of 1986 was not

Service Department

At any one time the Service Department of Aston Martin Lagonda at Newport Pagnell is likely to have as many as 100 cars within its walls – and without, as the company recently took on a 15,000 sq ft site, in part for storing vehicles due for long-term restoration.

In charge of the Department is Kingsley Riding Felce, who joined the company in 1976 and became General Manager of Service and Parts ten years later. 'The revival of Aston Martin's fortunes has seen a dramatic increase in the interest in early David Brown models – and in their value,' he says. 'This has given us the chance to maximise our opportunities as they have come along by carrying out modifications and restorations and doing a great deal of work in the Parts Department regarding the procurement of early DB material, everything from glass washer bottles to brake reservoir canisters. We have put a tremendous amount of time and effort into procuring these parts, not only to support our own Service Department, but also in order to sell them to restorers throughout the world.'

There is a careful blend of work in the Department, varying from a quick service – in Monday, out Thursday – to the complete restoration of a basket case which arrived in four tea chests with the simple request, 'Please can you turn this lot into a brand new DB4 convertible?' The answer is, of course, 'Yes, but at a price, which will be in the neighbourhood of £150,000.'

A full-blown restoration on a poorly DB5 will cost around £80,000, but many owners regard such an outlay as very good value. They are not interested in selling their cars; they simply want to have them rebuilt so they can go enjoying them for a long time to come. 'We have customers who have owned a car from new and want to go through the whole process of taking delivery again twenty-five years later,' says Kingsley.

The Service Department will restore any David Brown Aston from the DB5 onwards. Here a DB6 (with optional artwork) is all masked up awaiting new paint. In the background a Zagato drophead is in for its first service and a V8 undergoes inspection on a ramp

The tools of the trade about to go to work on a recently-removed David Brown six-cylinder engine

A measure of the increased interest in Astons is the fact that four years ago the Service Department comprised thirty people, whereas in 1990 it is up to fifty. Restoration is only a part of their business, as it involves very little turnover and ties up staff on long-term jobs. 'We try to balance our work between repairs, paintwork, mechanical servicing and restoration in order to get a regular turnover which we can measure on a monthly basis,' says Kingsley. 'My job is to make a profit for the Department and I have an annual target which has to be attained month by month.

'There are other firms doing the same work, so we have to be competitive, which means being efficient. On a restoration, for example, that includes steam-cleaning the vehicle properly, stripping it out, inspecting the parts, sand-blasting them and having them powder-coated and stored prior to being re-installed. We remove all the aluminium parts, shot-blast the chassis and then start the rebuild. We follow a complete set of disciplines.'

Only recently have Astons started advertising their Service Department by listing the spares available for early David Brown models, beginning with the DB5. They hold more than 117,000 different items. Due to the increased volume of work a full-time training instructor has been taken on in the Product Support Department and all Aston Martin Lagonda dealers are required to attend factory training sessions, to ensure that customers who cannot take their cars to Newport Pagnell get a thoroughly professional service from their dealer.

For many years now, the top-of-the-range Aston has been the Vantage, which has always been a very quick car. Not quick enough for some, however, as many owners have asked the company if there is anything that can be done to make it quicker still. To meet this demand, Astons have developed a 6.3-litre version of their 5.3-litre V8 and for a mere twenty-five grand will take your ordinary Vantage and turn it into a real road-burner by increasing the capacity by a full litre, fitting different cylinder liners, crankshaft, pistons, con rods etc, which greatly increase the venerable V8's torque and power to some 480 lbs/ft and 460 bhp. 'This keeps the customer extremely happy,' says Riding Felce, with some satisfaction.

'We also offer a handling package which includes different springs to go on the existing shock absorbers and front and rear anti-roll bars. We're only building six new Virages a week, so rather than wait two or three years for one of those, many customers want their old Aston turned into a new one. We're only too happy to oblige.'

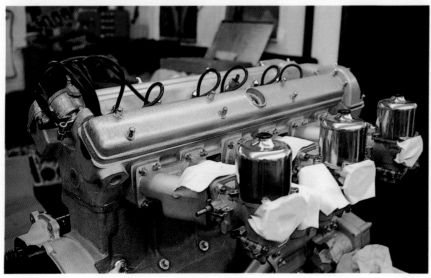

The heart of a thoroughbred – Tadek Marek's first engine for Aston Martin was the 3.7-litre straight-six which first appeared (in production form) in the DB4 at the end of 1958. With the arrival of the DB5 in 1963, the capacity had been increased to 3.9-litres and power upped from 240 bhp to 282, with the help of three SU carburettors

Marek's masterpiece was the 5.3-litre V8, which made its debut in the DBS V8 of 1970. Bosch fuel injection was fitted as standard. Here two engines await attention

One of the last of the twenty-five
drophead Zagato Astons sits on 'slave'
wheels until it is ready for its proper
ones

Above

'The impossible takes a little longer
. . .' This rusty hulk of a DB4
convertible (not, please note, a
Volante. This name did not appear
until the last of the DB5 chassis were
produced) looks set for the scrapyard,
but in fact it has been sent to Newport
Pagnell for a complete rebuild, which
will take a great deal of time at
considerable expense

Right

Q Car. Even James Bond's Aston needs
a service occasionally. The V8 saloon
was modified by the legendary 'Q' for
007's use in The Living Daylights. As
well as the rocket booster (seen here)
the Bond car was equipped with
extending skis and heat-seeking
guided missiles, extras which do not
appear on Astons' list of options

Above
*A V8 Volante – surrounded by pin-ups
– in the process of being re-trimmed*

Left
*Fore and aft bumpers in need of a good
polish*

Right
Catch 'em young! These are kiddicars with a difference – they cost £15,000 each! Twenty-five of these 4/7th scale Junior Volantes have been sold. Place your orders, please, for the Junior Virage Volante . . .

Left
A small section of Newport Pagnell's vast spares department, with some aluminium body parts awaiting delivery

AMOC and Astons' Racing Heritage

The Aston Martin Owners Club is one of the oldest one-make clubs in the world, having been founded in May, 1935 by that great enthusiast and amateur racing driver, 'Mort' Morris-Goodall. 'Mort's' infatuation with Aston Martins had begun a few years earlier when he bought an International. This was followed in 1931 by one of the works Le Mans racing cars, LM7, which he and Mrs 'Bill' Wisdom drove as part of the works team at Le Mans in 1933.

Having become great friends with A. C. Bertelli and finding everything to do with Astons so enjoyable, 'Mort' decided that there really ought to be a club for like-minded people. His friend, S. C. H. 'Sammy' Davis (who had driven in the works Aston team and managed it in 1934) felt the same way and mentioned the idea in *The Autocar* – of which he was Sports Editor – a couple of times. The result was that on May 25, 1935, some thirty enthusiasts foregathered, elected a committee and formed the Aston Martin Owners Club. Veteran town-to-town racer Charles Jarrott was elected President, 'Sammy' Davis Vice-President, and 'Mort' Morris-Goodall was appointed Honorary Secretary.

The Second World War brought to an end the Club's mainly social activities, but in 1948 another enthusiast, Dick Stallebrass, sent a letter to all known members informing them of his plans to get the Club going again, in the absence of Morris-Goodall, who was still serving in the Army. A meeting was held at the Royal Automobile Club in Pall Mall on March 5, 1948 and the AMOC was revived.

Nick Mason owns a handful of pre-war Astons including this one, former Team Car LM18, seen here on the grid for the St. John Horsfall Race. In 1935 it finished 12th at Le Mans and 5th in the Tourist Trophy. The following year it won a couple of races at Brooklands before being sold to France. Nick brought it back to England in 1977 and had it completely rebuilt at Morntane Engineering

Right
If it's Silverstone in June, it's bound to rain. A plastic sheet acts as temporary protection against the vagaries of the English weather

Below
Lined up in the Silverstone Paddock for the AMOC St. John Horsfall meeting, the Ecurie Bertelli cars enjoy the sunshine between rain showers. From left to right: a Mk II rebuilt to Ulster specification; Derrick Edwards' Ulster; Peter Hepworth's Mk II; Alex Pool's Ulster; Tony Bell's Le Mans; D. Elwell Smith's team car, LM10 and a Mk II

Charles Jarrott had died in 1944, so 'Sammy' Davis became the new President, with Dick Stallebrass as Honorary Secretary.

Sadly, Stallebrass was killed just four months later, when he crashed an Aston Martin in the Spa 24-hour race which, ironically, was won by the works Aston driven by St. John Horsfall and Leslie Johnson.

St. John Ratcliffe Stewart Horsfall was known to everyone as Jock. A remarkably gifted engineer and driver, he had started racing in 1934 with an International Aston which he prepared himself. Shortly after the war he was appointed assistant to Aston Martin's chief designer, Claude Hill, and the two of them covered many thousands of miles in what was to be the first of the David Brown Astons.

Tragically, Jock Horsfall's life was cut short in August, 1949, when he crashed Peter Bell's ERA during the final of the International Trophy race at Silverstone. Early the following year, the Aston Martin Owners Club decided to honour the memory of this much

This Aston began life in 1932 as a standard two-door Tourer. In 1967 its owner, E. A. Goble, shortened the chassis and fitted this 2/4 seater body. A magnificent conversion, the car won the Knebworth Concours in 1978

loved man by naming their very first race meeting after him. At Silverstone, on July 29, 1950, the St. John Horsfall Meeting was held and its main race of the day has celebrated Jock's memory ever since.

At that time the membership was approaching the 400-mark. Forty years on it is nearing 4,000, with members in over thirty countries. The St. John Horsfall Trophy Meeting remains the première event of the year, of course, but the Club now runs three race meetings every season at Brands Hatch, Silverstone and Oulton Park; a hillclimb at Wiscombe; three sprints – one at Goodwood and two at Curborough and two Concours at Silverstone and Stanway Park. All this activity is celebrated at the annual Ball and Prizegiving.

It is the St. John Horsfall Meeting that makes the AMOC the 'Keeper of the Flame' where Astons' racing heritage is concerned. Throughout the 1920s, 30s and 50s, the Aston Martin factory went racing with varied success, but all the owners of those years realised the value of competition in terms of improving the production cars and publicising the marque.

Left and above
This handsome Mk II 2/4 seater belongs to C. J. Sawday. That hood will keep some of the rain off, but the lack of side-screens could make life uncomfortable

Overleaf
The start of the main event of the day, the St. John Horsfall Trophy Race, with (left to right) Nick Mason in LM18; Robert Taylor (Le Mans, CG 6160); Judy Hogg (Ulster); Jim Young (Le Mans, APG 410) and the eventual winner Geoff Bishop in the famous Speed Model known as Red Dragon . . .

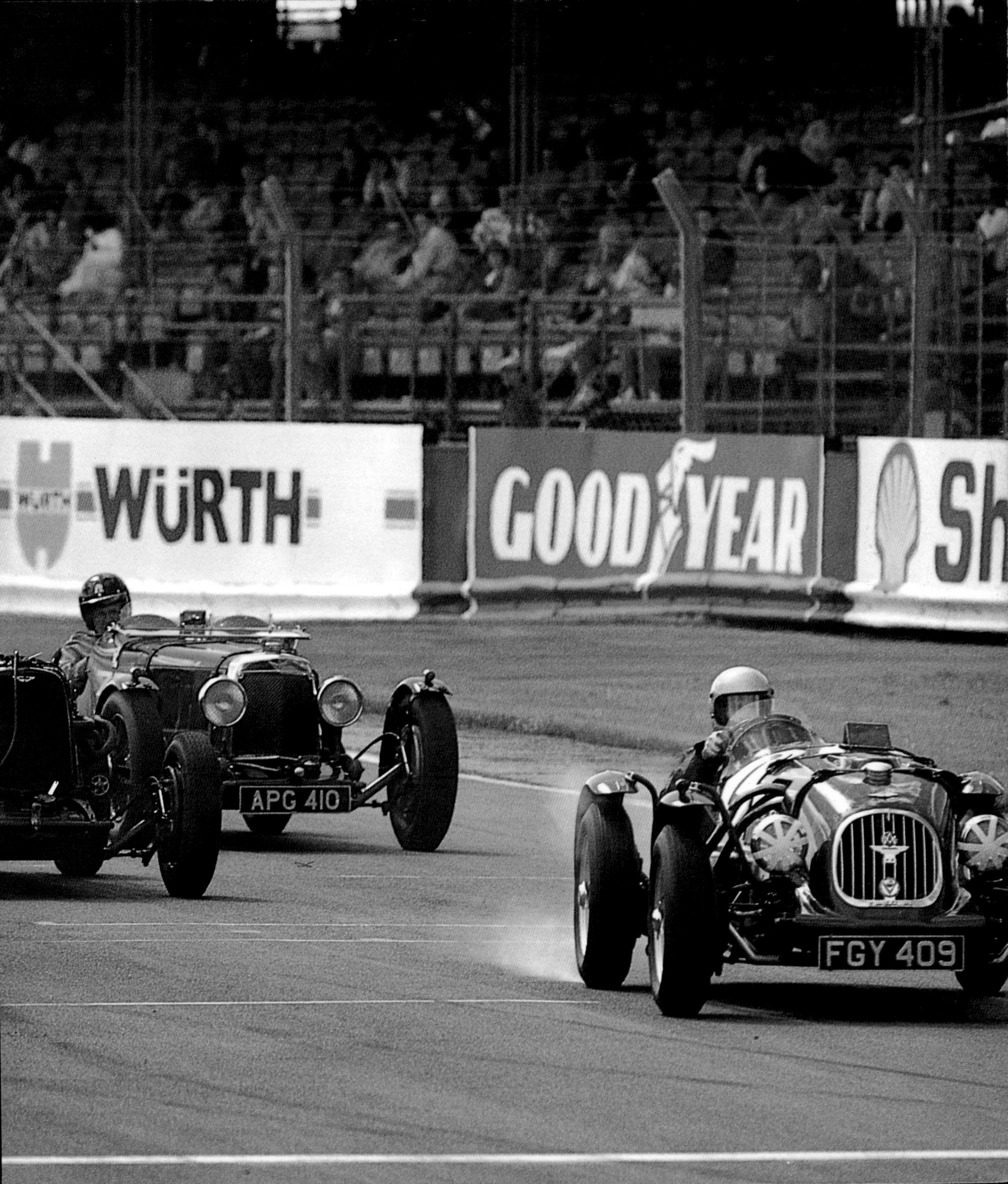
WÜRTH
GOODYEAR
APG 410
FGY 409

Geoff Bishop takes the winner's spoils after a fine win. His Speed Model was first raced in the 1936 Tourist Trophy by none other than Dick Seaman, but it retired. The following year it took part – without success – in the Mille Miglia and Le Mans, but won the Montlhéry Speed Cup and the Grand Prix des Frontiers in Belgium. The present body was fitted in 1950 and the car acquired the name Red Dragon at the same time. Since then it has been racing virtually every year and its immaculate appearance is the result of a complete re-build in 1987. A very famous Aston

Aston Martin was truly born of competition, for it was Lionel Martin's success with his modified Singer which brought him customers for similar cars and this, in turn, led him to design his own car. In the 1920s Lionel and his wife, Kate, raced Astons and one of the very first – known as 'Bunny' – became the first light car (that is, under 1500cc) to set a world record. In fact, it set ten at Brooklands in 1921, where it was driven by 'Sammy' Davis, Bertie Kensington Moir and Clive Gallop. It was Gallop who introduced the wealthy Count Louis Zborowski to Aston Martin and he paid for the firm to build two 1½-litre Grand Prix cars for the 1922 French GP.

Unfortunately, the race was for 2-litre cars with a minimum weight of 750 kg, so more weight had to be added to cars which were already giving away 500 cc to their rivals. Despite this, they were in fifth and sixth places when both were forced to retire with magneto problems. However, Zborowski went on to finish a fine second in the Penya Rhin GP the same year and again in 1923. The two GP cars were then sold and one was named Green Pea. It appears at AMOC meetings to this day.

During his ten years with Aston Martin, A. C. Bertelli built no fewer than twenty-two racing Astons. The first twenty bore the

*Judy Hogg in Derrick Edwards'
immaculate Ulster. In 1935 this car
finished 8th at Le Mans and won the
Targa Abruzzo at Pescara, where it
was driven by Count Johnnie Lurani*

prefix LM (although there was no LM13, for superstitious reasons)
and were all, reasonably enough, 1½-litre Le Mans models. The last
two cars were 2-litre Speed Models, which were built for the 1936 Le
Mans race under the new Gordon Sutherland regime.

The 1½-litre cars were always underpowered compared to the
opposition and seldom, if ever, in contention for outright victory.
However, they finished 3rd, 6th and 7th and won the Team Prize in
the 1934 Tourist Trophy race and came 3rd overall at Le Mans the
following year, when they again won the Team Prize in the TT,
finishing 4th, 5th and 11th overall. That was the last year the Aston
Martin factory was to go racing as a team until 1949.

In 1948, however, Jock Horsfall persuaded the company's new
owner, David Brown, to enter the Spa 24-hour race with the new
2-litre car Horsfall and Claude Hill had been working on for so long.
Rather against his better judgement, DB agreed and, to everyone's
surprise, the Aston won. That one-car entry could hardly be called a
team, but its success prompted David Brown to mount a proper team
effort in 1949. He set his sights on winning at Le Mans – the most
important motor race in the world at that time – and entered three
of his new DB2 models there. He also sent two cars to Spa.

The best they could do was 3rd and 5th in the latter event, but by now DB had caught the racing bug and realising that he had to do things properly he invited a certain John Wyer (whom he had noticed running AMOC member Dudley Folland's pit very efficiently at Spa in 1948) to become Astons' Team Manager for 1950. Wyer accepted, having first assured himself that he was to fill the post for only one year and could then look for a proper job. It was to be the start of a thirteen-year partnership.

In 1950 Astons achieved very little, but in 1951 they covered themselves in glory at Le Mans where the works DB2s finished 3rd, 5th and 7th overall, and 1st, 2nd and 3rd in the 3-litre class. Two privately-entered Astons were 10th and 13th. It was a marvellous result, but no works Aston was to finish at Le Mans again until 1955.

There were other successes, however. Aston Martins won all three Goodwood Nine Hour races, in 1952, '53 and '55. Peter Collins and Pat Griffith (who won the first Nine Hours in a DB3) won Astons' first World Championship event in fine style with the DB3S by defeating the Jaguar team in the 1953 Tourist Trophy at Dundrod and, earlier in the year, Reg Parnell brought his DB3 home fifth in the Mille Miglia, the highest place ever by a British car.

The 1954 season is best forgotten, it being a chapter of disasters. In 1955 the team found its way again with a new version of the DB3S, winning six races that season and finishing 2nd at Le Mans. The following year was something of an anti-climax, as the 3S was now in its fourth season and its successor, the DBR1, was only just ready in time for Le Mans, where it retired. The Moss/Collins 3S finished 2nd, however.

The DBR1 proved its worth in 1957, with a stunning victory against the full might of Ferrari and Maserati at the Nürburgring 1000 kms race, where it was driven by the remarkable Tony Brooks and Noel Cunningham-Reid, but all three cars failed at Le Mans. In 1958, sports car capacity was restricted to 3-litres, so Astons should have won the Championship that year, but they did not. A quite brilliant Stirling Moss repeated their Nürburgring victory, but once again, the cars failed at Le Mans.

Finally, in 1959, it all came good. Originally, Astons decided only to enter Le Mans and pour all their resources into winning the biggest prize of all, but they were persuaded to enter for Sebring, where they failed. Then Moss persuaded them to let him have a car for the Nürburgring where, with Jack Fairman, he scored yet another sensational victory. And then at last, at long last, David Brown's Astons won Le Mans, at the eleventh attempt. Roy Salvadori and Carroll Shelby brought their DBR1 home victorious ahead of team-

*Green Pea at speed. Some of the
earliest Astons were given very odd
names, such as Coal Scuttle, Bunny,
Razor Blade and Green Pea. The latter
(now owned and raced by Robert
Murray) is one of the two Grand Prix
Astons of 1922. This picture well
illustrates the little car's beautiful
proportions*

mates Paul Frère and Maurice Trintignant for an Aston Martin one-
two, and David Brown had fulfilled his greatest ambition.

To cap it all, the team then went to Goodwood for the final event
of the 1959 Sports Car Championship and, in a nail-biting race, won
the Tourist Trophy and the Championship. At a celebration dinner
shortly afterwards, David Brown announced that Aston Martin were
withdrawing from competition. It was the end of another era.

But not quite – in 1957 Astons had built a handsome Grand Prix car
which, unfortunately, they kept under wraps throughout 1958 while
they concentrated on the Sports Car Championship. Had the GP car
raced that year it would certainly have been competitive, but when it
did appear in 1959 the mid-engined GP car revolution was well under
way and the Aston was out of date almost before it turned a wheel in
anger. David Brown's Grand Prix effort ground to a dismal halt at the
end of 1960.

Two years later the team was back on the circuits, this time in the
Grand Touring category. The Astons – known as the Project Cars –
were based on the DB4GT and although they were very handsome
and quick, they were not quick enough to deal with the Ferrari GTOs
– except at Monza in 1963, when Roy Salvadori scored a memorable

win, beating Mike Parkes' GTO after a tremendous battle.

In 1967 Astons became briefly involved as engine suppliers to Eric Broadley's Lola GT project, but to no avail. It was not until the early eighties that the company dipped its toes in the racing waters again, by taking a hand in Robin Hamilton's short-lived Nimrod Group C racer. In 1989, however, Peter Livanos courageously put a very large sum of money on the table to back Aston Martin's AMR1 in the World Championship endurance races. Livanos' great ambition was to repeat Sir David Brown's Le Mans victory, but when the row between the AC de l'Ouest and FISA drove the 1990 race out of the Championship, he had no option but to close down his operation.

Sadly, it is unlikely that we shall see a works team of Aston Martins on the racetracks again in the foreseeable future. Astons' new owner, the Ford Motor Co., also owns Jaguar and as the latter company already had a well-established racing programme, Ford understandably saw no point in letting Astons race against it.

Which means that the best way of watching racing Astons in action is to visit one of the AMOC's events – preferably the St. John Horsfall Trophy meeting – where Astons of all shapes, sizes and vintages can be seen to their best advantage – at speed!

Among the most famous of all racing Astons, Geoff Parker's DB3S began life as one of the two, ill-fated Fixed Head Coupés (or saloons, as Team Manager John Wyer called them) which crashed comprehensively at Le Mans in 1954. Both were rebuilt as open cars for 1955 and registered 62 and 63 EMU. This one went on to finish second at Le Mans in 1955 and 1958

Q: When is an Aston not an Aston?
A: When it's a Lagonda.
Having bought the Lagonda company
soon after purchasing Aston Martin,
David Brown made several attempts to
revive the marque. The Lagonda
Rapide of 1961 (seen here) was
powered by a 4-litre version of the
DB4 engine and was essentially a four-
door Aston Martin intended to fulfil
David Brown's ambition 'to produce a
car which would be equally suitable to
drive or be driven in'. Although a
handsome carriage featuring de Dion
rear suspension and automatic
transmission, it did not find a market
and only fifty-five were built. This
example belongs to Brian Tustain

Overleaf

Below
The Mk III's special series DBD engine
with three SU carburettors produces
180 bhp. Although in Concours
condition, Ian MacGregor's car is used
regularly in the summer months

The Fixed Head Coupé is a very
elegant car, indeed. According to John
Wyer, Astons resorted to the FHC
when they found they could not sell a
number of Drop Heads.... Front disc
and rear drum brakes are well shown
here

Above and right
Frank Feeley's elegant lines have withstood the test of time admirably. The 3S is a Grand Touring car par excellence, but you'd need to send your luggage on ahead – that apparently large boot is almost entirely taken up with a fuel tank

Left
Beauty in full flight. Nick Faure in the lovely and very rare DB3S Fixed Head Coupé. Nineteen 'production' versions of the DB3S were built in 1955/56 and only three of them were FHCs. They were based on two similar cars built for Le Mans in 1954, where both were written off

Just as rare (or as common) as the production DB3S is the Zagato-bodied DB4GT, of which nineteen examples were also built. As these photos show, in many ways Zagato's design is a superb up-date of Feeley's – a fine compliment to the Englishman

You could not get away with such a number plate in this Britain

*When he was a huntin' man, Sir David
Brown commissioned the
coachbuilding firm of Harold Radford
to make him a shootin' brake on a DB5
chassis. It was such a success that a
further eleven were built. Rear door
swings upward — for the hounds,
don'tcha know?*

Above and left
Believe it or not, this fabulous beastie began life as a 1977 V8 Aston. In the intervening years its owner, David Ellis, has progressively modified it until there is precious little of the original car left. It now stands some ten inches lower than the standard V8 and weighs in at around 20 cwt, as against the standard car's 35 cwt. The V8 engine remains at 5.2-litres, but there the similarity with the production unit ends, for it now produces some 600 bhp. . . . Ellis has won over 200 trophies with his remarkable machine and reckons it is the world's fastest front-engined Aston

Left

Long-time AMOC stalwart David Holland has owned this Mk III drophead since 1967. The car has covered over 150,000 miles and will still cruise happily at around 100 mph on the Continent. David drives the Aston to every AMOC meeting of the year and it is seen here in the paddock at Brands Hatch

Above

This very smooth front-end treatment of an early DB2/4 is by AMOC member Peter Brown, who bought the car some fifteen years ago when it was in bits. His complete restoration included taking Frank Feeley's DB3S-style grille about as far as it can go. Mrs Brown restored the interior

Above and right
Immaculate DB2 Drop Head Coupé
shows Frank Feeley's superb styling.
The competition DB3 of 1952 was very
similar in appearance, but it did not
have this handsome interior.

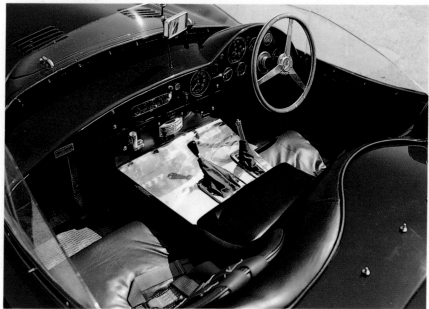

Above and left
Not what it seems. At first glance this exciting sports-racer might be taken for a DBR2 of 1957, but in fact it is a 1965 DB5 rebuilt to look like a DBR2. The handsome hybrid is the brainchild of AMOC members Edward and Heather Carter and was built by David Royle and Co., of Durham. Royle photographed and measured a real R2 before removing the bodywork of the Carters' DB5 and shortening its chassis to give it the same wheelbase as the racer. The original car was greatly modified to give it the appearance of the DBR2, but the Aston Martin DB5 Sports, as it is known, is not for racing. It must be a most exciting road car – providing it doesn't rain.

Having been shunted in its first race at Brands Hatch, Jimmy Wilson's DB4 is given first aid before its second

Marshall's Mounts. The ebullient Gerry Marshall appears regularly at AMOC meetings, driving Geoffrey Marsh's Marsh Plant Astons. This brutish V8 is entered, not surprisingly, in the class for 'Highly Modified Cars' and is outrageously quick, devouring virtually everything that dares compete against it. The single-seater is the DBR4, Aston Martin's belated attempt at a Grand Prix car for 1959. Had they raced it when it was first ready – in 1958 – it might have done some good . . .

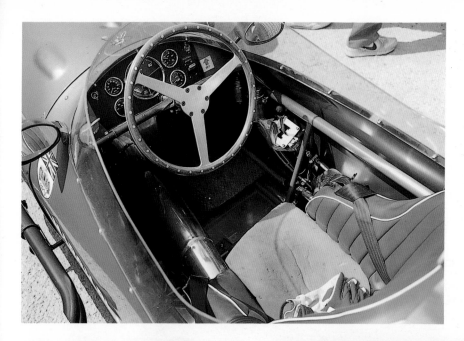

This beautiful Ulster is one of A. C. Bertelli's racers, LM15 – and thereby hangs a tale.... It was built in 1934 as LM11 and went to Le Mans with LM12 and LM14 (Bertelli would not have number 13). All three cars retired, so Bertelli had LM11 and 12 rebuilt and renumbered 15 and 16. In an attempt to better his Le Mans luck he had these cars – and a completely new one, LM17 – painted Italian red instead of British Racing Green and sent them off to compete in the Tourist Trophy, where they finished third, sixth and seventh overall and won the Team Prize. LM15 now belongs to Russell Hicks

Left
Leg show. Seen through some spectators' legs, Hugh Tyler leads Tom Hatfield down from Druids Hairpin in their DB4s

Below
Nick Mason in his former Team Car, LM18, rounding Paddock Bend at Brands Hatch

Overleaf
Tony Riseley in his International leads Chris Hudson's Ulster through Paddock

Ecurie Bertelli

To walk around Ecurie Bertelli's spotless workshop is to enjoy a brief lesson in the pre-war history of Aston Martin. Ulsters, Internationals, Le Mans and Speed Models stand on the red-painted floor, keeping company with one of the earliest Lionel Martin side-valve chassis and a 1922 Grand Prix car. Some are just in for servicing prior to their next race, but others are there for a complete rebuild, as Ecurie Bertelli is the world's foremost restoration company for pre-war Astons.

Run with quiet efficiency by Derrick Edwards and Judy Hogg, the firm has only been at its Buckinghamshire premises and under its evocative name since June, 1989, but it had its beginnings in London in 1975. Some good ideas begin as good ideas at the outset, but in this case, Derrick and Judy were not at first convinced that a specialist workshop dealing exclusively with pre-war Astons was a good idea at all. Were there really enough cars around with owners who would want them serviced and – better still – restored?

One who thought so was the man responsible for the good idea. Nick Mason is the son of documentary film-maker, Bill Mason, whose 'Shell History of Motor Racing' has become a classic. Bill also raced a Bentley in Vintage Sports Car Club meetings for a number of years, often against Derrick Edwards. Young Nick grew up to inherit his father's love of fine cars and his success with the rock group Pink Floyd has enabled him to enjoy his hobby in a way that the rest of us can only dream about.

In the early seventies, rebuilding pre-war Astons was something of a hobby for Derrick Edwards, whose 'proper job' at that time was running a BMC garage. Nick became a 'hobby customer' when he asked Derrick first to rebuild his International and then to find him a Le Mans. When he decided to go racing he requested that Derrick find an Ulster and also suggested that Derrick and Judy set up shop to

When Derrick and Judy Edwards started as Morntane Engineering in 1976 they were not at all sure that there were enough pre-war Astons around to keep them occupied. This is Ecurie Bertelli's workshop, fourteen years on . . .

The impressive front end of a long-chassis Mk II leads the eye to a case containing just some of the trophies won by Derrick Edwards over the years

A Mk II 2/4-seater of 1934, with an earlier International in the background

rebuild pre-war Astons full-time. Better still, he offered to finance the project and before you could say 'Le Mans' he had found and bought a property in London's Kentish Town.

'We were then looking after three cars,' recalls Judy, 'and we moved them into this vast premises where they looked quite lost. We didn't know how we were going to get enough customers to justify such a large area, but within a few months we were full to bursting!'

The new firm was called Morntane Engineering and it quickly established itself as *the* place for the re-fettling of pre-war Aston Martins. So good was Nick Mason's good idea that some ten years later a Japanese industrialist bought him out and Morntane Engineering moved north to Milton Keynes. The new partnership was not a success, however, and Derrick and Judy decided to go into business for themselves and the entire staff went with them, which speaks volumes for their abilities as employers.

The first Aston Martin badge, designed by Lionel Martin himself and used until about 1928. Until 1926, the name was hyphenated

Having used up all Martin's AM badges, A. C. Bertelli designed a winged badge of his own. This is the second of three versions, which was plated with the radiator shell

Immaculate engine bay of a long-chassis Mk II. Spare sparking plugs were a must

They found a new premises at Olney, in Buckinghamshire, providing 6,000 sq ft. They have added a mezzanine at the back, giving a further 3,000 sq ft which comprises their stores department and an engine test shop. Derrick and Judy head a team of seven mechanics, a lad and a driver and there are generally about fifteen cars in the shop at any one time, several of them from abroad.

Having found a new base, the company needed a new name and this time it was Derrick who had the good idea. He decided that Ecurie Bertelli would fit the bill admirably, as A. C. Bertelli was the inspiration behind so many pre-war Astons. Sadly, the great man is no longer alive, but Derrick and Judy managed to trace his son, who was delighted to lend his family name to the business. It could hardly be more appropriate.

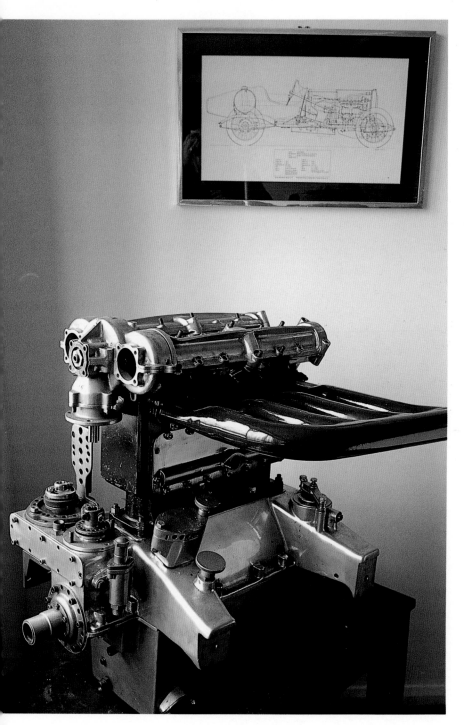

The 1.5-litre, twin-cam engine from the 1922 Grand Prix Aston Martin graces the Ecurie Bertelli entrance hall until the refurbished chassis is ready for it

Right
Brass plate on the GP engine gives both engine and chassis number as 1913

Below
Derrick Edwards is a long-time stalwart of the Aston Martin Owners Club and these are a few of his trophies

Edwards' 1935 Ulster, which he has owned since 1963 and raced consistently ever since. The late 'Bert' Bertelli spent many hours making the cockpit as comfortable as possible when the car was new. The hosepiping all round the edge is his original work, as is the gear lever knob – made from a rubber lavatory-pull!

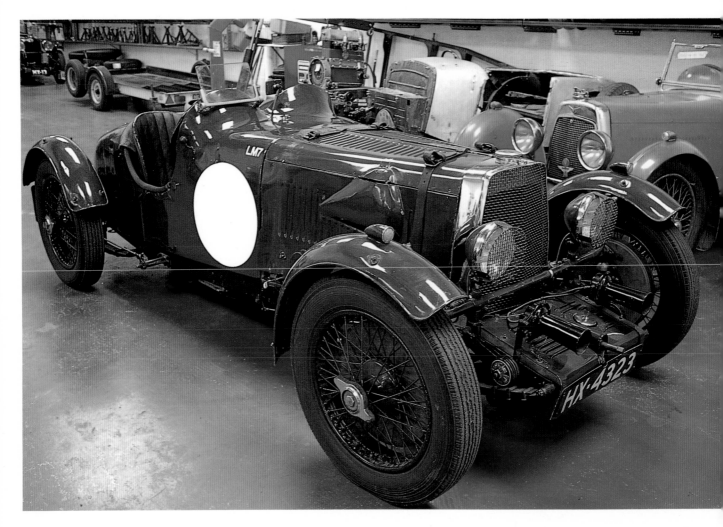

Bertelli built three new team cars for the 1931 season, chassis numbers LM5, 6 & 7. This is the latter, now owned by Nick Mason, one of the founders of Morntane Engineering. In 1931 the car finished 5th overall and 1st in class at Le Mans, driven by Bertelli himself and C. M. Harvey

LM7's twin-cowled dashboard. Above the switches on the left is a coloured guide to pit signals . . .

Above
*The four-cylinder, 1.5-litre engine
developed 70 bhp at 5,000 rpm*

Right
*The 1922 Grand Prix car, minus
engine, but nearing completion. 'It's
an absolutely wonderful car to drive,'
says Judy Hogg. 'Sounds like nothing
on God's earth with all those straight-
cut gears gnashing away!'*

Cockpit of the GP car. Believe it or not, two people shared this tiny space, as riding mechanics were carried in those days. Someone had to man the beer pump!

Above
A handsome, two-seater Inter, of 1930,
the earliest of the Bertelli Astons

Left
The engine bay is a magnificent
display of polished aluminium and
copper piping

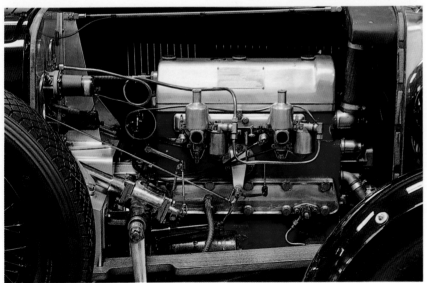

This International has a body made especially by Bertelli to look like an Invicta, at the original owner's request

The car has flared scuttles and a very
optimistic speedometer. It is in
original condition – a very hard-
worked Aston

*Notice that 'Aston Martin' with and
without a hyphen is written on this plaque*

Chassis of a Lionel Martin side-valve, 1.5-litre Aston Martin, circa 1924. The owner wanted its rebuild to be as original as possible, including, of course, the colour of the paintwork. A tiny patch of brown paint was found on one of the back plates and, happily, Bertelli's were able to match it. The colour of the boat-tailed body will be the original buttery yellow

Monterey

Every year Steve Earle, creator and organiser of the Monterey Historic Automobile Race Meeting at Laguna Seca Raceway, in California, selects a manufacturer to be the Featured Marque at his event. In 1989 he chose Aston Martin, to co-incide with the 30th anniversary of their victory at Le Mans.

Chairman Victor Gauntlett took the opportunity to present a remarkable display centred upon that victory by building a replica of Astons' Le Mans pits in Laguna Seca's paddock and rounding up four of the five DBR1 sports cars – including the race winner – that the factory campaigned in the late fifties under the team management of the legendary John Wyer. Even more remarkable, perhaps, was the fact that all six drivers who took part in that race thirty years ago were still alive and well and Victor Gauntlett was able to invite them to Monterey – with the team's patron, Sir David Brown – for a truly historic re-union.

The Aston Martin Owners Club was also there in force and had its own Concours and Gala Dinner in the town of Monterey, with members coming from all over America and Europe. Held every August, the Monterey Historic meeting is one of the finest of its kind in the world and everyone with an interest in historic racing should make a point of attending at least once.

Jack Fairman tries the 1959 Le Mans-winning DBR1 for size. Jack was in the winning team, but not the winning Aston, which was driven by Roy Salvadori and Carroll Shelby

Right and overleaf
*Robert Fergus took two Astons to
Monterey in 1989, this beautiful 1935
two-seater Ulster and the DB4GT in
the background. The Ulster's cockpit
is slightly over the top, everything –
including the gearchange linkage box
– being trimmed in leather*

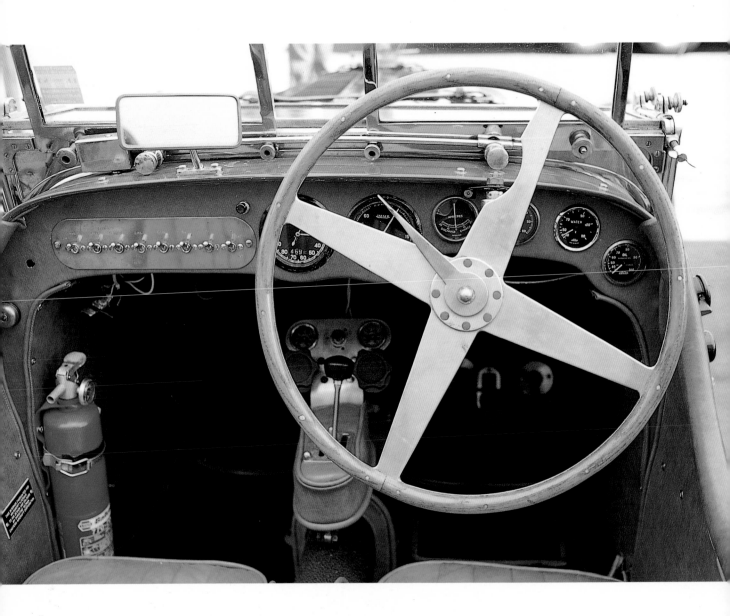

Right and overleaf
Tetsuya Takahashi's immaculate 1.5-litre twin cam was a Team Car built for Humphrey Cook to drive in the 1925 Junior Car Club's 200-mile race at Brooklands. Cook crashed on the first lap, due to brake lining failure. In those days you drove on the handbrake, which operated the drums by a cable. In front of the handbrake is the gear lever. You needed a strong right arm in the twenties

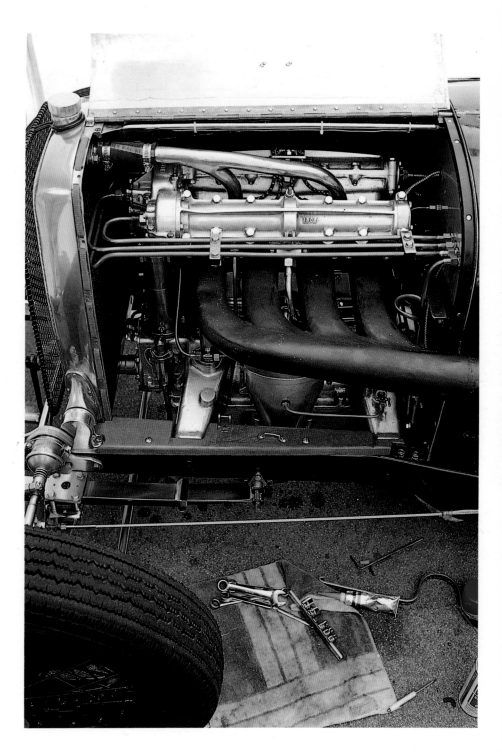

Right
Eric Traber of Switzerland owns this beautifully restored DB3S. Chassis number DB3S/5, it began life with an experimental fibre-glass body and was used by David Brown as a road car until commandeered by the works in 1954 and raced until 1956, when it was sold. It had no major successes, but won some minor races in the hands of Reg Parnell, Roy Salvadori and Stirling Moss

Overleaf
Willie Green stylishly bends DBR1/4 into one of Monterey's corners. This car finished second at Le Mans in 1959, in the hands of Paul Frère and Maurice Trintignant

Previous page and right

Mike Salmon indicates that he is bringing the DBR2 into the pits. The R2 is the R1's big brother and almost identical in appearance. One major difference is that the R2's exhaust exits under the passenger door, whereas that of the R1 exits under the driver's – and tends to deafen his right ear! The R2 had a 3.7-litre engine when it appeared in 1957, a de-tuned version of which went into the DB4. The beautiful lines of this car (and the DBR1) were the work of Astons' Chief Racing Designer, Ted Cutting

Right
A bashful V8 hides from the sunlight

Overleaf
Project 212 was Astons' first attempt at a rather half-hearted come-back to racing in 1962. Based on a DB4GT, it had a 4-litre engine and made its debut at Le Mans, where Graham Hill gladdened the hearts of all Aston fans by leading the first lap in fine style, but the car was aerodynamically unstable and hard to handle. It eventually retired with a hole in a piston. Today Project 212 is owned by the President of the AMOC, Viscount Downe

Right
Only two of these 1956 Touring-bodied
DB2/4 Mk II Spyders were built. This
beauty is now owned by American
AMOC members Whit and Lynne Ball

Overleaf
Home, James! Michael Sharp's
pristine but pug-ugly C-type Aston of
1939 is homeward-bound. Ugly or not,
it won 2nd in Class at the AMOC's
Monterey Concours

Psst! Wanna buy a badge, Guv?